The Hidden Value in a Broken Sword

OMAR'S journey

Written By

Emersen Parker

Design + Layout

Damon Kidwell

71 Design Team

ROUTES TO WEALTH MEDIA

ROUTESTOWEALTHMEDIA.COM

Beyond financial education, "Omar's Journey" is designed to be a visceral immersive experience.

We take a first principles approach to equip young readers with necessary foundational knowledge.

Our aim is to inspire children to see themselves as active participants in shaping their future by combining meaningful education and compelling storytelling.

In the grand city of Córdoba, there lived a respected silk merchant named Tariq, who had once been a brave warrior.

In his home, there was a gleaming commemorative sword hanging on the wall. A relic from his days defending the Moorish Empire. Omar, his curious young son, loved to hear stories about his father, who he affectionately called "Baba". Tariq would regale his son about his own adventures, Omar would always imagine himself wielding that sword.

Omar's mother, Layla, often watched him with a knowing smile. She knew the boy's imagination ran wild with dreams of distant battles. But she also knew how much the sword meant to Tariq.

One day Omar returned home from his lessons to find himself all alone. His father, still at the marketplace and his mother, tending the garden as she often does. Omar, left to his own devices and imagination, takes his father's sword from the wall.

Realizing the weight of the sword, he gathers all of his strength as he slices the blade through the air, vanquishing his imaginary enemies in battle.

Control

But in his excitement, Omar lost control of the sword. It slipped from his hands and crashed to the ground with a loud clatter.
The once-proud blade was now cracked, damaged by his carelessness.

Damaged

Layla came rushing in at the sound.
Her face softened as she saw the broken sword and Omar's expression.
"Oh, Omar,"
she said quietly,
"your father will be heartbroken."

Heartbroken

When Tariq returned home and saw the broken sword, his gaze was heavy but calm. "Omar", he said, "you've made a big mistake."

Omar, ashamed, stammered, "I'm sorry, Baba. I didn't mean to break it."

Tariq sighed, "Omar, you are going to have to pay for this sword to be repaired. In order to repair the sword we must journey to Palermo and Cairo, where two master swordsmiths can restore it.

Omar did not protest, but he knew he did not want to leave. He wanted to stay home with his mother, Layla, and attend the Summer Fest and have fun.

He spent the entire night trying to think of
a way to avoid the journey
and stay for the festival.

So the next morning,
in a last-ditch effort to avoid his responsibilities,
he gathered items from the house -
sacks of salt, jars of olives, and baskets of grain.

He approached his father
and said, "Baba, take these.
You can trade them to fix the sword.
That way, the repairs are paid for
and I don't need to go."

Fix
the
Sword

Tariq looked at the goods and shook his head with a knowing smile. "Omar, this is not how the world works. You can't simply offer goods to escape responsibility. The master swordsmiths will only accept money for their time and services."

Omar Frowned.
"Why Can't We just use these Goods to Trade?"

"Because," Tariq explained, that's not money. "Carrying large sacks of salt and olives across the seas is impractical, as these items are abundant and carry very little value to the swordsmiths."

Tariq, noticing how his response left Omar sad and confused, said to Omar, "It is time you learn what money is and the principles that govern it."

"Money-gold dinars and silver dirhams were created to make trade easier. These coins represent trust, and acceptance by all, they are a medium of exchange, a unit of account, they are divisible, have a limited supply and act as a store of value.

The swordsmiths won't accept sacks of salt-they'll accept these coins because their value is recognized all around the world."

Layla, who had been listening quietly, nodded at Omar. "Your father is right. There are things you must learn that go beyond bartering simple goods. Gather your things and prepare to go with your father."

Reluctantly, Omar realized his mother and father left him no choice, he had to go.

The next morning, Omar and Tariq set sail for Palermo. They encountered a fierce storm. The water was rough, lightning flashed, and the sea roared, tossing the ship from side to side. Omar clung to the railing, his heart pounding in his chest. The crew struggled to keep the ship steady, and for hours they fought against the wind and rain.

Finally, after what felt like an eternity, the storm subsided, and the ship reached the shores of Palermo. Having arrived at the harbor with their ship safely docked in the bustling port, they began to disembark. But as they stepped onto solid ground, Omar couldn't shake the memory of the storm that had nearly claimed their lives. He thought of the sailors, each one working frantically to keep the ship afloat.

Some had braved the high mast to adjust the sails, clinging to ropes as the wind threatened to sweep them into the sea. Others had bailed water from the deck, struggling in the heavy rain. "Baba," Omar asked, "do all the sailors get paid the same? Some had much harder jobs than others."

Tariq smiled, recognizing his son's growing understanding. "This brings us to another principle, Omar: unit of account. Money helps us measure the value of different types of work. Each sailor's job has a value based on the skill, danger, and effort involved. Those who took on the riskiest tasks, like climbing the mast during the storm, might be paid more than others. Money lets us fairly measure and pay for the work each person does."

Omar nodded, seeing how money could reflect not just the cost of goods but the worth of hard work, skill, and bravery. The sailors coins would be a reminder of the value they create, just as his father's sword was a reminder of his.

Visited the Master Swordsmith

THE DUO VISITED THE MASTER SWORDSMITH WHO EXAMINED THE DAMAGED BLADE. "IT WILL TAKE TIME AND SKILL TO REPAIR THIS SWORD," THE SWORDSMITH SAID. "THE COST WILL BE HIGH, BUT I CAN DO MY PART TO RESTORE IT.

Bustling Full of Life

Tariq agreed on a price, and they left the sword to be repaired. With time on their hands, they decided to take a walk through the city. The streets of Palermo were bustling and full of life. Omar watched street-performers, merchants, and people trading goods and coins. He noticed that people handed over coins, and sometimes received different smaller coins in return.

"Baba," Omar asked, "why do people receive smaller coins back when they pay with a large one?"

"This is called divisibility," Tariq explained. "Not everything costs a large gold dinar. Some things, like a loaf of bread or a basket of fruit, are much cheaper than a horse, for example. Money is made so it can be divided into smaller units like silver dirhams or copper coins, so you don't need to pay more than necessary.

Divisibility allows us to assign value for a range of goods and services, from a pinch of salt to a fleet of ships."

Omar realized how practical money was. It could be broken down, just like portions of food, to fit different needs.

Necessary

WITH THE SWORD WORK COMPLETED IN PALERMO, TARIQ AND OMAR SET SAIL ONCE AGAIN, THIS TIME FOR CAIRO. THE JOURNEY WAS LONG, BUT THEY WERE DETERMINED. ALONG THE WAY, THEY STOPPED ON A SMALL ISLAND TO RESUPPLY THEIR FOOD AND WATER. THE ISLAND WAS INHABITED BY A SMALL VILLAGE OF FISHERMEN WHO LIVED SIMPLY OFF THE LAND.

Here We Don't Use Money

TARIQ OFFERED ONE OF THE FISHERMEN SILVER IN EXCHANGE FOR SOME FISH, BUT THE MAN SHOOK HIS HEAD. "HERE, WE DON'T USE MONEY," THE FISHERMAN SAID. "WE TRADE FISH FOR WOOD, OR SALT FOR GRAIN. WE DON'T HAVE A NEED FOR SILVER HERE."

We Don't Have a Need for Silver Here

Lesson in Acceptance

Omar was confused. "Baba, why didn't the man accept the coin, couldn't he use it later to trade?"

Tariq explained, "This is a lesson in acceptance. In most places like Córdoba, Palermo and Cairo, people accept coins because they trust they can use them elsewhere. But in smaller, isolated places, people may rely on bartering because they don't need to exchange or trade with as many people in distant lands. Money only works when people agree to accept it."

"So the salt I was going to give you, Would have been of value?"
Tariq sheepishly grins, turns his hands up, laughing at Omar's wit.

Fully rested after sailing the calm seas, the pair arrive in Cairo. Tariq and Omar enter the master swordsman's shop. The master swordsmiths come from a line of famed craftsmen. His ancestors developed an unparalleled skill set having been taught by a master who was given access to the libraries of Alexandria.

Sailing the Calm Seas

These highly sought after abilities were then passed down from generation to generation. The combination of his knowledge and impeccable work made it possible for Tariq's sword to be returned to its former glory.

Arrive in Cairo

Knowledge

"OMAR, WE HAVE TRAVELED FAR AND AT GREAT EXPENSE TO REACH THIS SHOP. THERE WERE MANY CRAFTSMEN ALONG THE WAY. BUT NONE WITH THE ABILITY TO DO THE WORK WE REQUIRED.

THIS KNOWLEDGE AND MASTERY IS IN LIMITED SUPPLY, MAKING IT HIGHLY VALUABLE. MONEY, LIKE THIS KNOWLEDGE, MUST HAVE A LIMITED SUPPLY IN ORDER TO MAINTAIN IT'S VALUE."

While the swordsmith finished the restoration, Tariq and Omar walked amongst the pyramids of Giza and the Sphinx. Omar gasped with amazement, "Wow Baba!" After the two gazed upon the magnificence of the pyramids they returned to the swordsmith.

The sword was fully repaired and ready. With it's gleam brighter than ever, Omar reached to grab the sword, but Tariq quickly snatched it before Omar could do so. Omar looked up at his father and grinned. "Baba, I had to try." Tariq clinched the sword and bid farewell to the swordsmen.

As they prepared to sail back to Córdoba, Omar curiously asked his father, "Baba, can anything be used as money, as long as it satisfies the principles?"

Tariq smiled at his son's curiosity. "That's a good question, Omar... Yes, money has and will come in different forms." Tariq holds out both of his hands to show Omar they are empty.

"But not everything can be used as money. Money, in the form of gold or silver, are not only rare, but very durable."

Tariq reaches one hand behind Omar's ear and magically produces a silver coin

Rarity and Durability

"A coin made with these precious metals 1,000 years ago, would be just as pure today as it was then. That rarity and durability makes it an excellent store of value. This is part of the reason why gold...

Store of Value

AND SILVER HAVE BEEN RECOGNIZED AS MONEY FOR OVER 4,000 YEARS." OMAR REACHES FOR THE COIN BUT IT DISAPPEARS INTO THIN AIR., TARIQ SMILES. "BABA!". TARIQ JESTS WITH OMAR AS THEY SAIL TOWARDS THE SUNSET.

WHEN THEY RETURNED HOME TO CÓRDOBA, THE SWORD, NOW FULLY RESTORED, WAS PLACED BACK ON THE WALL. OMAR HAD LEARNED MORE THAN HE EVER IMAGINED ON THE JOURNEY

NOT JUST ABOUT SWORDS AND BATTLES, BUT ABOUT THE SIX PRINCIPLES OF MONEY: MEDIUM OF EXCHANGE, UNIT OF ACCOUNT, DIVISIBILITY, STORE OF VALUE, LIMITED SUPPLY, AND ACCEPTANCE.

Sitting together by the fire that night, Layla smiled at her son. "You've learned so much, Omar. Not just about fixing mistakes, but about how the world works."

Omar nodded. "I understand now. Money isn't just coins, it's the thread that connects people across the world."

The End

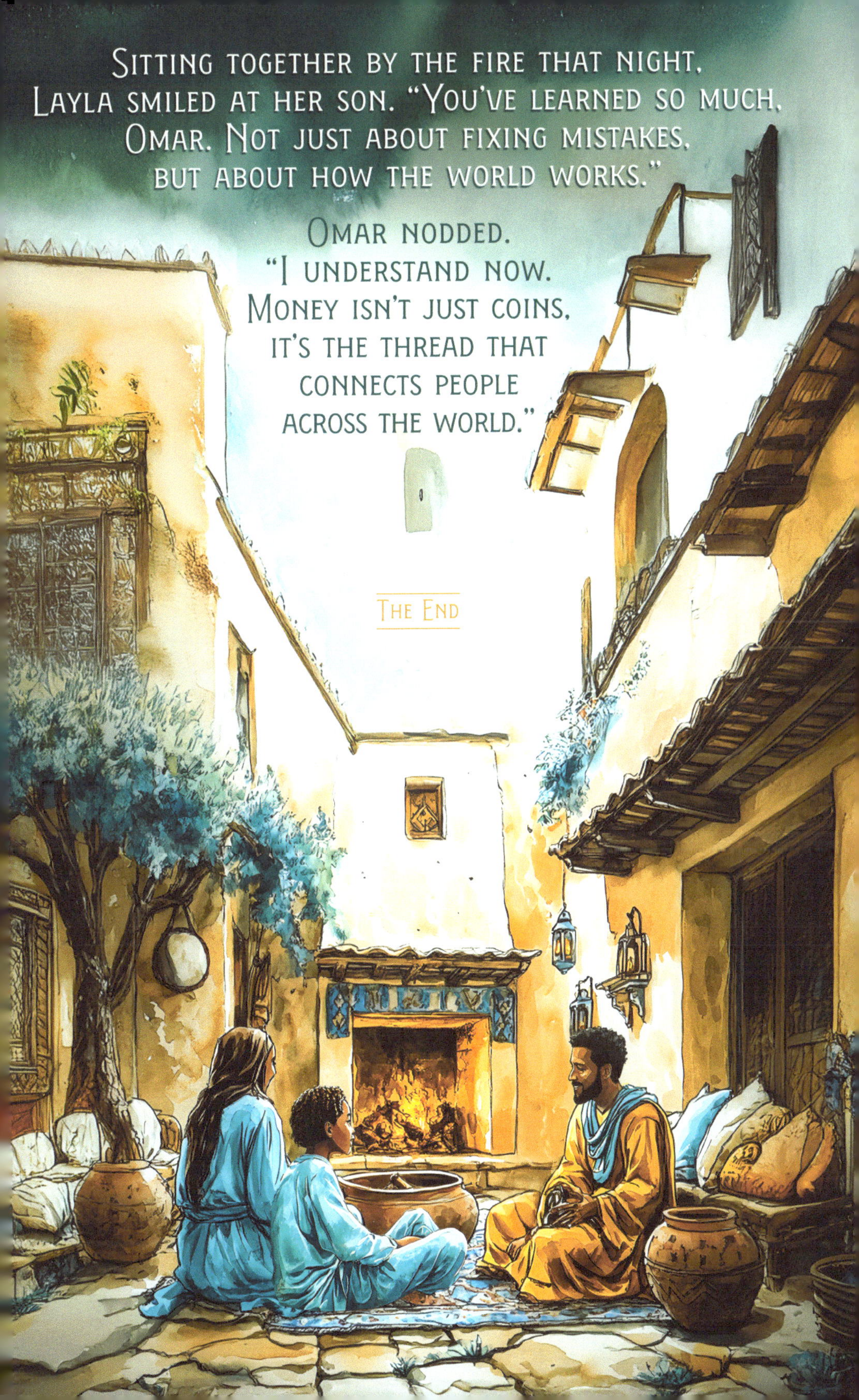

"Money Doesn't Grow on Trees, But it Grows on Intelligent Minds"

- MATSHONA DHLIWAYO

www.ingramcontent.com/pod-product-compliance
Lightning Source LLC
LaVergne TN
LVHW051155210926
848486LV00005B/280